STOCKHOLM

Göran Brämming Gallery AB

ISBN 919746213-6

"Af Chapman" hostel in Skeppsholmen

INDEX

City Hall

*C*ity of climate contrasts, of water and light in the summer, ice and darkness in the winter, the **capital of Sweden** has such evocative charm that it is considered the "**Venice of the North**". Its medieval center, which sprang up around the little island of Stadsholmen, is still the heart of **Gamla Stan** (the Old City), but today the city has expanded to the fourteen islands that separate the Baltic Sea from Lake Mälaren, connected by bridges and ferries. Merchant boats and warships have plied the narrow channel since medieval times, and were often attacked by pirates. It was this very need to defend this important communication route and protect the inhabitants from being plundered that produced the birth of Stockholm as a fortified city around a nucleus of 11th century pile-dwellings. General **Birger Jarl**, who unified the country and was regent to the throne of Sweden from 1248 to 1266, was responsible for the fortress. Its present-day name, which means "island of tree trunks," is probably derived from the defensive barricades built to control the inlet.

In **1252 Stockholm was already a city**, protected by walls and a castle that was never breached despite numerous assaults. By the end of that century it became the largest city in the country and an important commercial interchange due to agreements reached with the Hanseatic League, which controlled the transport of copper and iron to Europe. During the 14th century, various kings of Denmark attempted to occupy it, and a struggle erupted here between supporters of the Kalmar Union, which united Sweden, Norway and Denmark under a single king, and advocates of independence. In November 1520, when Sweden recognized the sovereignty of Christian II of Denmark, the final resistance was stamped out in the sadly famous Bloodbath of Stockholm. One of the few nobles who escaped the slaughter, **Gustav Vasa** led a revolt and seized the throne of Sweden on June 6, 1523, now celebrated as a national holiday.

The **Vasa dynasty** made Sweden a great European power, a position it held for the entire 17th century. Stockholm, which became the official capital of the realm in 1634, grew in importance until it became a political, cultural and administrative center. Under Christina of Sweden (1632-1654), Sweden's scientific and philosophical culture rivaled that of the rest of Europe, and her successor, Carl X Gustav (1654-1660), brought it to its height of power with the conquest of Denmark. After the disastrous defeat against Russia (1709), Stockholm went into a decline, and the city was

Sentry box of the Royal Palace

View of Strandvägen from Skeppsholmen

brought to its knees by an economic recession and a series of famines, epidemics and fires. Little by little the monarchy gave up its absolute power until it became a form of democratic government; political power is now in the hands of Parliament. Beginning in the last twenty years of the 19th century, the Industrial Revolution marked a demographic upsurge that changed the face of Stockholm with the creation of new working class neighborhoods, while the social conquests of the 20th century led Sweden to become one of the most advanced countries in Europe.

Today Stockholm has once again become an important economic and financial center and home to prestigious artistic and scientific academies and the Nobel Foundation.

*A*lthough devastated by numerous fires between the 17th and 19th centuries, the city was spared by the two world wars due to Sweden's declaration of neutrality. Its medieval imprint can still be seen in the **Gamla Stan** district, located on an island in the center of the city, alongside Renaissance era edifices, imposing royal residence and new, practical modern districts. The imposing city hall tower with its three golden crowns is a symbol of the city. Of its monuments, **Drottningholm Castle** and the south cemetery, **Skogskyrkogården**, have been placed on UNESCO's World Heritage list. But beyond its architectural beauty, Stockholm owes its charm to the numerous canals and inlets that separate the islands and peninsulas, its bridges, the balance between green and urban areas and its enviable geographical position, nestled among parks and hills that look out over the great archipelago.

Panoramic view from the top of the City Hall Tower

Stockholm

14

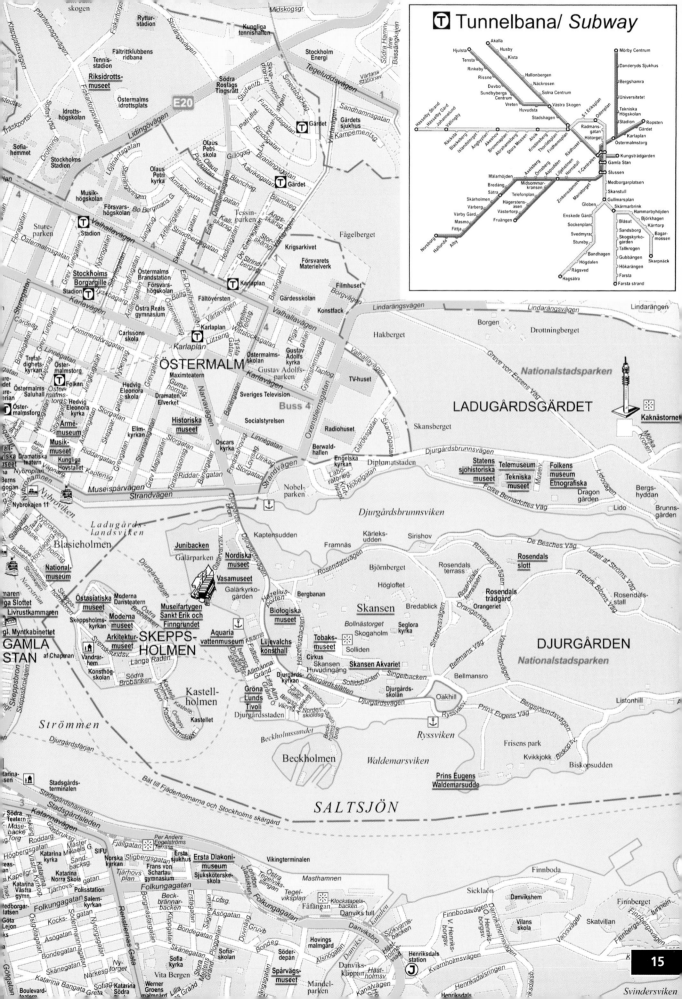

SOUTH STOCKHOLM

*T*he south end of Stockholm is formed by **Södermalm Island**, which overlooks the wide bay of Riddarfjärden (Knights' Fjord) to the west and the bay of Saltsjön to the east. Once home to artists and workers, today it is an elegant residential area full of shops, hotels and restaurants, and is steeped in an evocative atmosphere that makes it almost a city unto itself. Old and modern architectural styles blend here: wooden houses from the first half of the 18th century, hotels and inns built on old ships anchored at the port, and elegant streets dotted with pubs and clubs that fill with people at night, with **Söder Torn** standing out on the skyline.

Connected to Gamla Stan, the northern section of Södermalm, called **Slussen** (dry dock), is where you're likely to see pleasure boats sailing by. **Söder Mälarstrand**, the road that skirts the bay of Riddarfjärden, runs west to the island of **Långholmen**, connected by two bridges. Once home to prisons, it is now a working class district where the old royal prisons are the site of a hotel and museum.

Coming to Södermalm, the first attraction we see

Söder Mälarstrand

is **Katarinahissen**, the steel lift built in the 1930s that takes you 38 meters above the old streets of Mosebacke. This district contains one of the most important theaters in Stockholm, the **Södra Teatern**, rebuilt and opened in 1859 after a fire in 1853. The **Mosebacke** terrace offers a broad panorama of the city. Or you can walk up along **Monteliusvägen**, a pedestrian area lined with benches and panoramic areas. At the foot of Mosebacke hill, a 17th century edifice contains the **Stockholms Stadsmuseum**, the municipal museum dedicated to the history of Stockholm. The St. **Katarina Church** in Högbergsgatan was built in the 17th century on the ruins of some old chapels, by order of King Carl X Gustav, who entrusted the design to the famous

St. Katarina Church

Stigbergsgatan

architect Jean de la Vallée (1620-1696). Seriously damaged by fire in 1990, the edifice is an example of restoration using the original construction techniques. Recently, a **new mosque** was built next to the church, to emphasize the cosmopolitan character of a city that mixes languages, culture and religions from all over the world.

Proceeding east, you'll come to two of the most characteristic streets in the district: **Fjällgatan**, a little cobblestone road that climbs up the hill, flanked by picturesque wooden buildings that are for the most part reconstructed, with the original street lamps jutting from the walls, and **Stigbergsgatan**, whose fully restored wooden houses are the last original ones left, making them the city's oldest historic legacy.

*M*edborgarplatsen *(City Square), the pulsing heart of Södermalm, is surrounded by Neoclassical palaces. Not far from Medborgarplatsen, in Fatbur Park, is* **Söder Torn***, a soaring residential building with an octagonal design. It was completed in 1997 by architect Henning Larsens Tegnestue: after much controversy, the original*

The Stomatol insignia at Klevgränd

design by Ricardo Bofill, which had called for a 40 story building, was reduced to 24 floors. The district around **Södra Station**, west of Medborgarplatsen, is in an area that was once occupied by Lake Fatburen, which was drained around the mid-1800s in order to build the new train station (1860). More than a century later, during Stockholm's great urban renewal in the 1980s, the neighborhood was transformed into a residential area. Spanish architect **Ricardo Bofill** was entrusted with designing a large residential complex and the tall building that stands in the center of **Fatbur Park**. The main building, in Neoclassical style, has a façade that curves around an open space 180 meters in diameter, running two blocks south and three west. In the center of the boulevard that traverses the park, adorned with various sculptures, there is a fountain and a pond.

On the south side of the city, with good subway service, is the enormous four building complex that hosts sporting events and large concerts: the **Ericsson Globe, Annexet, Hovet** and **Söderstadion**. The Ericsson Globe, the largest spherical structure in the world, was opened in 1989 to host the world cup in ice hockey - an extremely popular sport in Sweden -

Söder Torn

and since then has been a stage for European and world class competitions, performances by stars like the Rolling Stones, Bruce Springsteen and U2, and appearances by world famous personalities such as John Paul II, the Dalai Lama and Nelson Mandela. Designed by the Berg Architects studio to hold 16,000 spectators, the structure was completed in the record time of two and a half years. There is an extremely popular shopping mall around it that is almost a city in itself, with stores, hotels, restaurants and banks.

The Ericsson Globe

Skeppsbron

THE OLD CITY: GAMLA STAN

M ost of the medieval city stands on Stadsholmen Island, connected by bridges to the smaller islands of Riddarholmen and Helgehandsholmen, with Parliament located on the latter. **Gamla Stan**, the center of Stockholm, is a maze of cobblestone streets, arches and stairways, most of which are closed to traffic. The narrowest lane, less than a meter wide, is **Mårten**

Stortorget

21

Stortorget

Trotzig Gränd, with a steep 36-step climb past 16th century houses and picturesque establishments. Two of these buildings were owned by the German merchant Traubzig, giving the lane its name. Closed for over a century, it was reopened to the public in 1945. Another lane is *Gåsgränd* (Goose Lane), which runs into Västerlånggatan, a narrow street full of shops, restaurants and ethnic establishments.

"S:t Göran and the dragon"

Mårten Trotzigs gränd

The German church soars above the roofs of Gamla Stan

Gåsgränd

"Den Gyldene Freden" restaurant in Österlånggatan

*T*he 13th century cathe-dral is located in the upper city. Known as **Storkyrkan**, it has a baroque façade with 15th century Gothic style interior. It contains exquisite artistic works, including a silver altar and a large bronze candelabra, the painting entitled **Parhelion**, with the oldest known view of Stockholm, and the wooden sculpture of "**S:t Göran and the Dragon**" by sculptor Bernt Norke. An true late Gothic masterpiece, the work was completed in 1489 to commemorate the battle of Brunkeberg (1471) against the Danes. A bronze replica can be seen in Köpmanbrinken, in front of the Royal Palace.

THE ROYAL PALACE

*T*he old 13th century fortress, transformed into a royal residence by the first kings of Sweden, was destroyed by a fire in 1697 and then replaced by the current palace, designed by architect Nicodemus Tessin the Younger and built between 1697 and 1754, the year in which Adolf Frederik transferred the court there.

*T*he large apartments of the **Royal Palace**, the official residence of the king, are where most official royal ceremonies take place. Between ceremonies, the state rooms are open to the public.

*T*he **festival ball** has the oldest furnishings in the palace, dating back to the late 17th century. Among other events, the sumptuous hall hosts official receptions in honor of state visits.

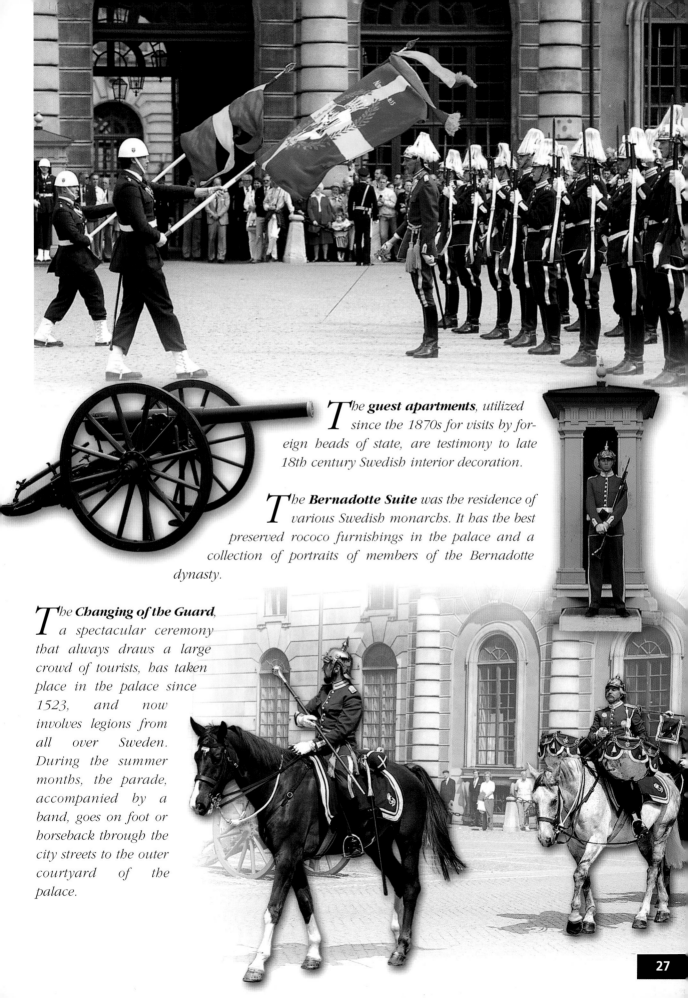

*The **guest apartments**, utilized since the 1870s for visits by foreign heads of state, are testimony to late 18th century Swedish interior decoration.*

*The **Bernadotte Suite** was the residence of various Swedish monarchs. It has the best preserved rococo furnishings in the palace and a collection of portraits of members of the Bernadotte dynasty.*

*The **Changing of the Guard**, a spectacular ceremony that always draws a large crowd of tourists, has taken place in the palace since 1523, and now involves legions from all over Sweden. During the summer months, the parade, accompanied by a band, goes on foot or horseback through the city streets to the outer courtyard of the palace.*

Karl XI Gallery

*P*resent-day **king Carl XVI Gustav** *ascended the throne upon the death of his grandfather Gustav VI Adolf in 1973. Even though it is the official residence of the king, the Swedish royal family has not lived in the Royal Palace since 1981. The current family is comprised of* **King Carl XVI Gustav**, **Queen Silvia**, *and their three children -* **Crown Princess Victoria, Prince Carl Philip** *and* **Princess Madeleine**.

*S*ome of the 10 royal palaces near Stockholm *include* **Drottningholm Palace**, *the* **Chinese Pavilion, Tullgarn Palace, Rosersberg Palace** *and* **Gripsholm Palace** *in* **Mariefred.**

His Majesty King Carl XVI Gustaf and Her Majesty Queen Silvia

The royal yacht Vasaorden was built in 1774. It was damaged by a fire in 1921, then rebuilt in 1922-23. Its appearance in the waters around Stockholm often signals visits from foreign heads of state or important ceremonies for the royal family.

The Victoria Hall

*The royal palace contains various museums: the **Tre Kronor Museum** offers visitors a taste of medieval history. The old Tre Kronor fortress was destroyed by a fire in 1697, sparing only the north wing. The ring walls, which were begun in the 14th century, and the 16th century masonry arches make up the palace's present-day walls and roof. The objects salvaged from the flames and found during excavation work give us an idea of daily life in the palace.*

*The **Gustav III Museum of Antiquities**, opened to the public in 1794, is one of the oldest museums in Europe. Most of the sculptures in the museum were acquired by Gustav III during his trip to Italy in 1783-1784.*

The **Livrustkammaren**, located in the palace's cellars, presents the history of the Swedish kings, and displays armor and weapons produced for Gustav Vasa and the horse Streiff that Gustav II Adolf rode during the battle of Lützen.

*L*ower down, in the vaults, are the **Treasury Rooms**, where the most important symbols of the Swedish crown are kept. In the past, they were removed from their coffers only for official ceremonies, but since 1970 crowns, scepters, keys to the kingdom and swords have been displayed. The oldest item is Gustav Vasa's 16th century sword.

Treasury Rooms

Panoramic view from Skeppsholmen

DROTTNINGHOLM PALACE

*D*rottningholm Estate*, immersed in a pristine natural setting on an island on Lake Mälaren, contains sumptuous Drottningholm Palace, which since 1981 has been the official residence of the royal family. Located about ten kilometers from the center of Stockholm and accessible from the capital by ferry in little over an hour, parts of the residence are open to the public.*

The magnificent palace, construction of which began in 1662, is almost entirely in baroque style, with additions from the 18th-19th centuries and gardens inspired by the court of Versailles. The estate includes a **splendid court theater** from 1766, which is in perfect condition, and the **Chinese Pavilion**, the summer residence of King Gustav III (1771-1792). The Palace, Theater and Chinese Pavilion are on UNESCO's World Heritage list.

PARLIAMENT AND SAGERSKA PALACE

U ntil 1905, during the bicameral period, the Swedish Parliament had its seat in Fleming Palace on Riddarholmen Island. It was then moved to a new building on Helgeandsholmen, but in 1971, due to lack of space, it had to be expanded, connecting the old palace with the one that had originally held the National Bank. Upon completion of the work in 1983, the new seat was

Auditorium Hall in Parliament

Sagerska Palace

opened to hold sessions of the unicameral Parliament in an enormous, practical, modern hall with the walls entirely paneled in light birchwood. In the large inner halls, which still have interesting early 20th century architectural elements, including some imposing granite columns and marble staircases, there is an exquisite collection of paintings. Parliament still has some offices in Gamla Stan, which are connected by a network of underground passageways, while other government buildings are located in the City. In particular, these include the **Chancellery,** the seat of the **Secretary of State**, which occupies an elegant late 19th century palace, and the Prime Minister's residence, located in **Sagerska Palace**, a linear edifice with a decorated façade, whose beautiful, artistic, wrought iron balconies overlook the Norrström canal.

Parliament

THE NOBEL PRIZE

*T*he **Konserthuset**, located on Hötorget Square, is the city's concert hall and since 1926 home to the Stockholm Royal Philharmonic Orchestra, a magnificent neo-Classical palace that architect Ivar Tengbom designed based on a Greek temple, in order to "erect a temple of music not far from the Arctic Circle." Restored in the 1970s and 1990s, outside it stands the **Orpheus Fountain** statue group by artist Carl Milles. Milles used the lofty columns that run along the façade of the palace, which faces the marketplace, to symbolize the strings of an enormous lyre played by the gigantic Orpheus. The same sculptor created the four marble statues that adorn the entry to the Konserthuset.

In addition to hosting concerts and internationally famous soloists, the Konserthuset also hosts the annual Nobel Prize awards ceremony.

One year before his death, **Alfred Nobel** wrote a will that would immortalize his name by creating the **Nobel Prize**, which became the most important honor in the world.

According to Alfred Nobel's wishes, each year 5 prizes are awarded to "those who, during the pre-

ceding year, shall have conferred the greatest benefit on mankind": a prize for physics, chemistry, physiology and medicine, literature and peace. The executor of the will is the Nobel Foundation.

*T*he **Stockholm Concert Hall** is famous throughout the world, because this is where the Nobel prizes are awarded on December 10 of each year, on the anniversary of Alfred Nobel's death. During the official ceremony, the king personally gives each winner a certificate and gold medal in the presence of the winners' families and royalty, as well as representatives of the Academy of Sciences, Karolinska Institutet and the Swedish Academy, and numerous members of the Swedish government, Parliament and the diplomatic corps. The Nobel Peace Prize is awarded in Oslo by the Nobel Committee, which is part of the Norwegian Parliament.

*T*he evocative ceremony in the Concert Hall is followed by a sumptuous **banquet** served in the Blue Room of the Stockholm City Hall, with about 1300 guests served by about 200 waiters.

*N*obel Prize winners always stay in the most prestigious hotel in Sweden, the **Grand Hotel**, which overlooks Strömmen canal right across from the Royal Palace. Founded in 1874 by the French cook Régis Cadier, who had been the head cook for the court of Oskar II, over the years it has been renovated numerous times, but many of its original elements have been preserved, such as the great hall inspired by the Hall of Mirrors in Versailles and the Winter Garden, a banquet hall that seats 800 persons.

DOWNTOWN STOCKHOLM

*I*n the center of the City, **Sergels Torg** is a two-level square, one for pedestrians and one for automobiles, on which stands the **Kristalverticalaccent**, a glass and steel obelisk by the sculptor Edvin Öhrström (1972). The entry to the cultural center (**Kulturhuset**), with its long glass façade, also stands on the square. The palace, opened in 1974

and renovated in 1999, is
the work of celebrated architect
Peter Celsing, who made his mark on post-
World War II Stockholm by designing numerous
churches and subway stations, the latter for the
most part finely decorated by over a hundred
Swedish artists. In addition to being the site of the
City Theater, the center has a packed cultural
calendar, and its auditorium hosts various kinds
of performances.
The City is also a shopping paradise; you can start
from the
Åhléns department
store in Sergels Torg, take a
walk to the Kungshallen indoor markets
on Hötorget square, in front of the
Konserthuset, and end at the luxurious
Sturegallerian shopping center in

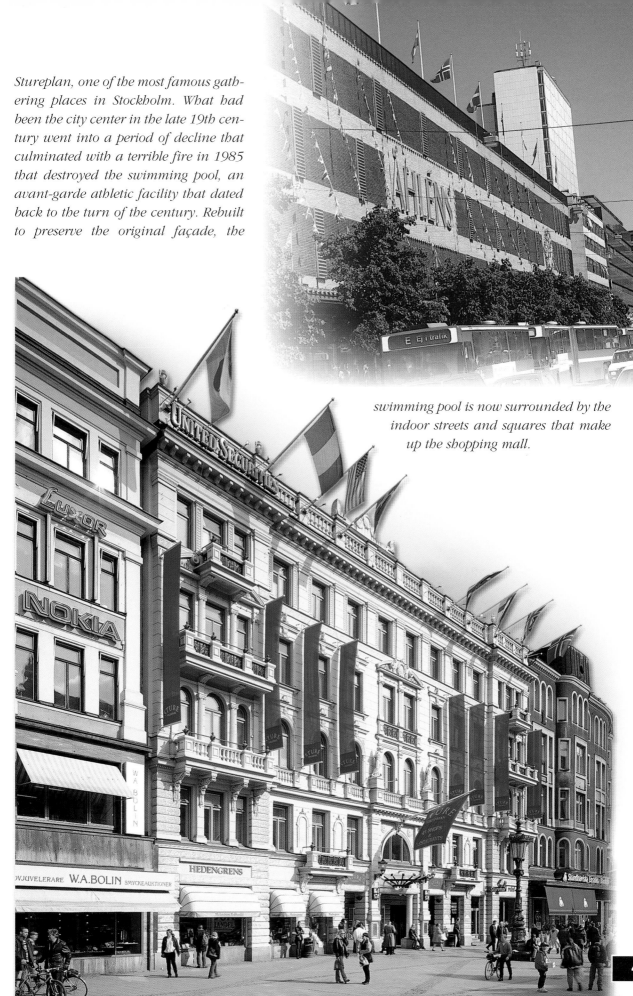

Stureplan, one of the most famous gathering places in Stockholm. What had been the city center in the late 19th century went into a period of decline that culminated with a terrible fire in 1985 that destroyed the swimming pool, an avant-garde athletic facility that dated back to the turn of the century. Rebuilt to preserve the original façade, the

swimming pool is now surrounded by the indoor streets and squares that make up the shopping mall.

ARCHIPELAGO

*O*ne of the classic excursions around Stockholm is a trip through the archipelago. To the east, the sea is dotted with over **24,000 islets** and reefs with a singular natural beauty; the nearest, about a half hour from the city, are the **Fjäderholmarna** islands. To the west are the islands of Lake Mälaren, which have been inhabited since ancient times and were used as a shelter by the Vikings. Of particular interest are Björkö Island, which is on UNESCO's World Heritage list,

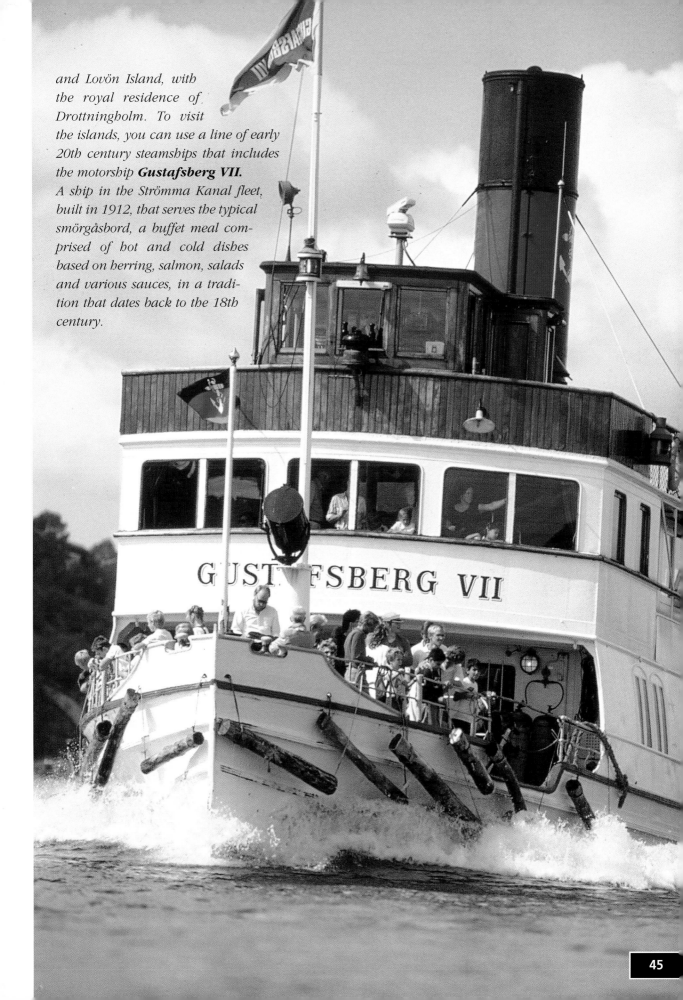

and Lovön Island, with the royal residence of Drottningholm. To visit the islands, you can use a line of early 20th century steamships that includes the motorship **Gustafsberg VII**. A ship in the Strömma Kanal fleet, built in 1912, that serves the typical smörgåsbord, a buffet meal comprised of hot and cold dishes based on herring, salmon, salads and various sauces, in a tradition that dates back to the 18th century.

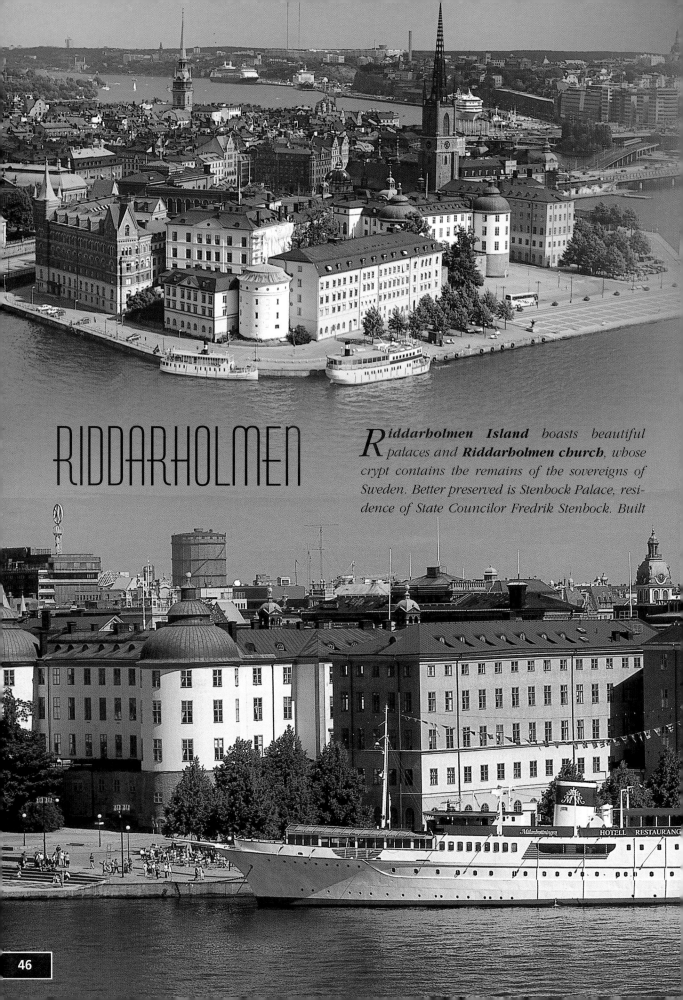

RIDDARHOLMEN

*R*iddarholmen Island boasts beautiful palaces and **Riddarholmen church**, whose crypt contains the remains of the sovereigns of Sweden. Better preserved is Stenbock Palace, residence of State Councilor Fredrik Stenbock. Built

in the mid-17th century, it was restored numerous times, and contained first the State archives and then the Supreme Court. It still has its original stucco ceilings, period floors and grand staircase designed by Nicodemus Tessin the Elder. Another noble residence from the same period is **Wrangel Palace**, across from Birger Jarls Torg, with the statue of the legendary founder of Stockholm. Along with tower known as Birger Jarls Torn, the south tower built into the palace is one of the last vestiges of the defensive walls built around the island by Gustav Vasa in 1530. Later expanded, in the late 17th century Wrangel Palace was home to the royal family for a few decades and now is the seat of the Court of Appeal. One of things that distinguishes Riddarholmen is the luxurious yacht **Mälardrottningen**, formerly owned by the American millionaire Barbara Hutton, and now transformed into a hotel. In the reception, the walls are paneled in dark wood with brass trim, while the cabins are divided into rooms; the restaurant, located on the main deck, offers a magnificent view.

CITY HALL

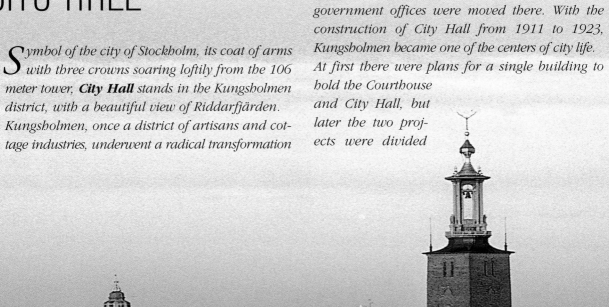

*S*ymbol of the city of Stockholm, its coat of arms with three crowns soaring loftily from the 106 meter tower, **City Hall** stands in the Kungsholmen district, with a beautiful view of Riddarfjärden. Kungsholmen, once a district of artisans and cottage industries, underwent a radical transformation between the 19th and 20th centuries, when the new courthouse was built (1911) and various government offices were moved there. With the construction of City Hall from 1911 to 1923, Kungsholmen became one of the centers of city life. At first there were plans for a single building to hold the Courthouse and City Hall, but later the two projects were divided

and entrusted to architects Carl Westman and Ragnar Östberg, leading exponents of the Romantic school.

Construction, completed in 1923, was begun on occasion of the 400th anniversary of the entry into the capital of King Gustav Vasa, who restored the kingdom of Sweden.

On the outside, the edifice has an imposing red brick façade and a long portico that faces the terraces-garden overlooking the water, with access to Riddarfjärden along a stairway flanked by two allegorical statues by Carl Eldh depicting, respectively, Song and Dance. One of the columns that dot the portico is adorned by a bas-relief by Christian Eriksson depicting the artist Carl Larsson painting a view of the capital from the other side of the Riddarfjärden.

Terrace on the water

On the east side stands a massive square tower surmounted by a gilded spire; a lift takes you to the middle level, where there is an interesting **Tower Museum** *that explains the history of City Hall. From the top of the tower there is a broad panoramic view of Riddarholmen and the Old City.*

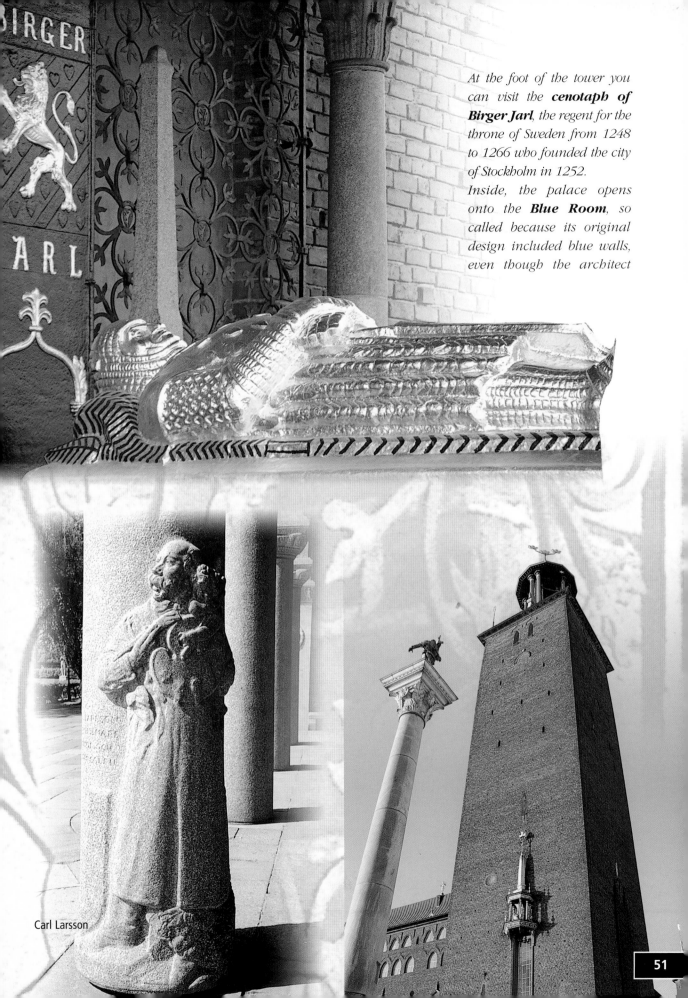

At the foot of the tower you can visit the **cenotaph of Birger Jarl**, the regent for the throne of Sweden from 1248 to 1266 who founded the city of Stockholm in 1252.

Inside, the palace opens onto the **Blue Room**, so called because its original design included blue walls, even though the architect

Carl Larsson

Detail of mosaic on wall of the Gold Room

The Blue Room

later decided to make them of decorative brick. This is the largest hall in the palace, where each year a banquet is held in honor of Nobel Prize winners. It has the largest pipe organ in Northern Europe, with over 10,000 pipes.

In the center of the palace, the stupendous **Gold Room** has walls decorated with mosaics made of 18 million pieces of very thin glass and gold leaf, the work

of Einar Forseth (1892-1988). An outstanding piece is the **Queen of Lake Mälaren**, a magnificent mosaic that covers the entire wall, portraying the city of Stockholm as a queen on a throne as she receives homage from East and West.

On the east side of the building is the Borgargården, a courtyard that overlooks the **Council Hall**, with its walls decorated with geometric motifs and a highly original ceiling whose structure with false openings looks like the open sky, as in Viking homes. The furnishings in the Council Hall were chosen during the 1920s by artists Maja Sjöström and Carl Malmsten, among others.

Dotted by a row of slender, austere twin columns, the **Prince's Gallery**, which runs along the south side of the palace, is currently used as a hall for official city receptions. The splendid view of Riddarfjärden from the windows is also depicted in the beautiful fresco that runs along the opposite

Prince Gallery

wall, *The City on the Water*, painted by Prince Eugene (1865-1947).

*T*he antechamber of the festival hall, the **Ovale,** was created especially for the Tureholm tapes- tries, woven in Beauvais, France, around the end of the 17th century. Civil marriage ceremonies are performed here every Saturday afternoon.

Council Room

Tower Museum

The Ovale

NATIONAL CITY PARK

*T*he Swedish capital was the first city in the world to open a national city park, the **Ekoparken**, which extends from Ulriksdal Palace in the north to the Fjäderholmarna islands in the south, connecting areas that were once royal hunting reserves and are now dotted with historic palaces and museums. A classic guided tour includes a visit to the Royal Palace, Gamla Stan, and Hagaparken, the English-style park on the northern edge.

The vast natural area of Ladugårdsgärde, commonly referred to as Gärdet and now transformed into a park named after Alfred Nobel, has palaces where the Swedish radio and television offices were transferred in the 1960s and 1970s. One of the typical period buildings is the imposing **Kaknästornet**, built in 1967 by

Bengt Lidroos and Hans Borgström as a radio transmission center. One hundred and fifty-five meters high, it now contains a restaurant that offers a spectacular view of the city.

Not far from the Museum of Natural History, the **Bergianska Gardens**, a botanical museum managed by the Bergius Foundation, include over 9000 species

from all over the world. The **Edvard Andersons Växthus greenhouses** have year-round exhibits of Mediterranean flower species and rain forest and desert plants.

Overlooking the bay of Edsviken is the elegant, baroque **Ulriksdal Castle**, named after the last niece of Queen Mother Hedvig Eleonora. Built in 1644 based on a design by Hans Jakob Kristler, the palace belonged to one of the most powerful men of the country, the royal marshall Jakob de la Gardie, who sold it to the queen in 1669. Remodeled numerous times, it still has some 17th century decorations, but the façade we see today is from the following century, as is the court theater, which is still used for summer performances. Transformed into a hospital in 1821, around the mid-19th century the palace was modernized by Carl XV, who added to the collection of artwork and had it decorated by the great designer Carl Malmsten. In addition to the rooms used as a residence, you can visit the orangerie, a late 17th century construction designed by Tessin the Elder and transformed into a sculpture museum, and the large park created during the same period.

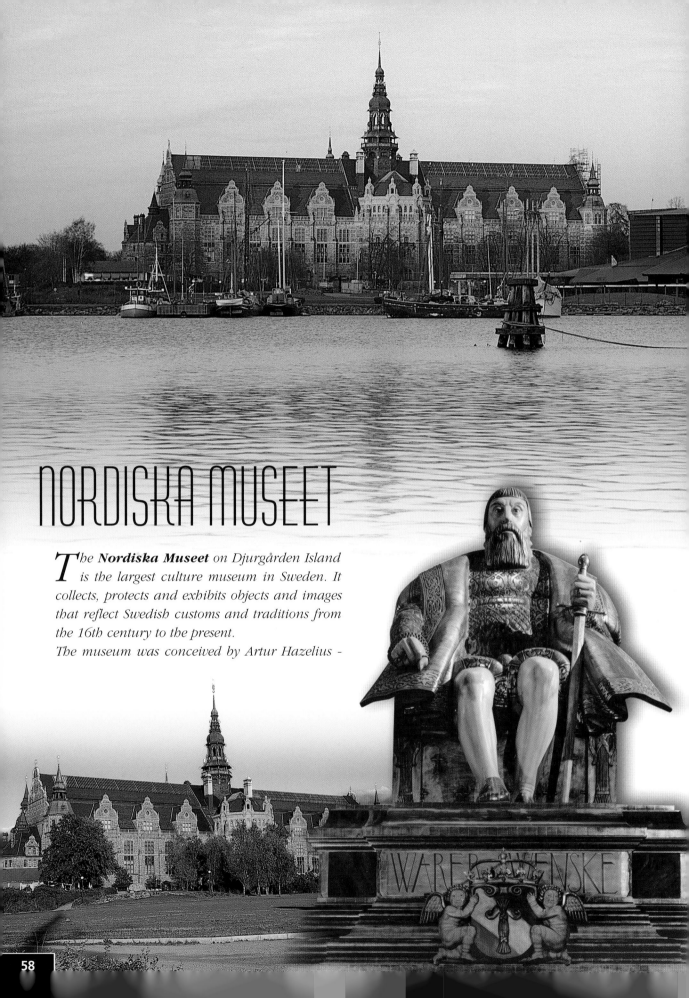

NORDISKA MUSEET

*T*he **Nordiska Museet** on Djurgården Island
is the largest culture museum in Sweden. It
collects, protects and exhibits objects and images
that reflect Swedish customs and traditions from
the 16th century to the present.
The museum was conceived by Artur Hazelius -

who also created the Skansen Museum - and opened in 1907. During a trip to Dalarna in 1872, Hazelius realized that the old peasant culture was vanishing, and he decided to

Gustav Vasa (1496-1560), the king who unified the country and freed it from Danish domination. Completed in 1925, it is the work of Carl Milles, who sculpted it from oak: according to legend, the front of the statue contains a piece of oak planted by the king himself. The wooden statue was then painted and gilded.

Some of the various exhibits include fashion items that run from 18th century to punk styles, **table settings from the 16th to 20th centuries**, old toys, furnished rooms with interiors from 1870-2000, and old dollhouses. The Nordiska Museet has a permanent exhibit dedicated to **August Strindberg** (1849-1912), Sweden's most famous writer, including original manuscripts, photographs and sixteen paintings by Strindberg.

try to pass down what was left for posterity. During the trip, he thus purchased an old woolen skirt that became the first item in the museum's collection, which now includes 1.5 million objects.

The architect Isak Gustaf Clason designed the museum in the style of Scandinavian Renaissance palaces, inspired by Danish examples. After the Ericsson Globe, the great hall is the largest secular hall in Sweden, measuring 126.5 m in length and 24 m in height.

At the entrance is the **colossal statue of**

VASAMUSEET

The **Vasa Museum**, built to hold the **royal warship the Vasa**, the world's only example of a completely outfitted 17th century warship, was opened to the public in 1990. The pride of the Swedish navy, the Vasa was built during the reign of Gustav II Adolf. It was the most powerful warship ever built, but - probably due to an improper distribution of weight - it did not even complete its maiden voyage and sank in the port of Stockholm in August 1628 while it was heading to a naval base south of the capital, where 300 soldiers were supposed to have embarked.

Thanks to the work of the marine archaeologist **Anders Franzen**, who began research in the 1950s, the **vessel was recovered in 1961** after almost four years of work required to lift the ship from the sea floor and tow it to a dry dock. Of course, lengthy reconstruction work was necessary for the corroded parts, but the hull was intact, preserved by the low saline content of the water, as were the 6 sails, which had not been raised when the ship sank.

Equipped with 64 cannons, the Vasa had 150

crew members who, along with the soldiers, were all sleeping on the bridge. The captain's cabin was decorated with paintings and wood sculptures and also had glass windows, a luxury for a ship of that time.

Aft, there are numerous sculptures, which must have once been brightly painted, including a row of soldiers. In the prow, next to smaller sculptures, is a lion that weighs over 450 kg. In all, over 700 carved wooden pieces were recovered, most of them the work of sculptor Mårten Redtmer.

The museum also includes various everyday objects, copper coins, hats and other personal effects found on board.

In addition to the ship, the museum has various permanent exhibits. For example, one is dedicated to the recovery of the Vasa and one to the construction of 17th century warships.

Outside, a **botanical garden** lets you admire the medicinal plants and aromatic herbs cultivated at that time.

Two period ships are anchored in front of the museum and can be visited in the summer: the first is the Swedish **ice breaker Sankt Erik**, launched in 1915, and the other is the **lightship Finngrundet**, built in Gävle in 1903, which was moored in the shallows of Finngrund with a crew of eight men during the months when the water was ice-free. Retired in 1969, when the lightship was replaced by an automatic fixed lighthouse, it was transformed into a museum.

GRÖNA LUND

*D*jurgården Island has the oldest and most exciting amusement park in Sweden - **gröna lund Tivoli** - where people have been enjoying themselves since 1883. An excellent way to reach the park is to take the **Djurgårdsfärjan boat** from Slussen to Allmänna Gränd on Djurgården. Gröna Lund is quite old. It dates back to a small amusement park created in 1883 by Jakob Schultheis, who wanted to name it after a tavern that stood on the site, Gröna Lund, which literally means "green grove." Every year the park attracts a million visitors of every age who come to enjoy one of the 25 attractions, go to the variety show, or sample succulent dishes in one of the numerous restaurants.

SKANSEN

*A vast area of Djurgården is occupied by the **Skansen** open air museum built by Artur Hazelius in 1891, reconstructing peasant life in Sweden. One hundred and fifty wooden houses, farms and storehouses from all over the country were transferred here, from the poorest dwellings with straw and turf roofs to the elegant estate of Skogaholm, a 1680 residence that comes from the city famous for its iron work. The urban section reproduces artisan shops from 19th century Stockholm. In the center of Skansen is **Seglora Church**, built in 1729-30, which has*

a very old pulpit and rich interior decorations. Not far off, we can also visit the **House of the Soldiers**, originally from the Småland region in southeast Sweden, with its tree trunk walls and sod roof. The park also contains the pavilion that belonged to the philosopher and scientist Emanuel Swedenborg (1688-1772). Skansen is also a large zoo that contains many of the animals that live in the northern forests, running free in their natural habitat. The aquarium and terrarium attract swarms of visitors every year; two of the main attractions are the Brown Bear Den and the Seal Tank.

Every year, Skansen celebrates one of Sweden's most popular festivals, **Midsommar**, which falls on the first weekend of the summer solstice, when the sun shines all day and night. A pole decorated with flowers and leaves is set up in a field, with dances, singing and the traditional banquet around it.

PRINS EUGENS WALDERMARSUDDE

*T*he former residence of Prince Eugene (1865-1947), **Waldemarsudde Castle**, built in 1903-1905, was transformed into a museum upon his death to conserve the paintings he collected as well as his own work. Considered one of the leading landscape artists of his generation, he

did many of the paintings now on display at the Stockholm City Hall (*The City on the Water*), the Opera Theater and the Dramatic Arts Theater. Waldermarsudde Palace, designed by architect Ferdinand Boberg with the **collaboration of the prince himself**, and completed in 1905, contains several of his most famous works, including *Spring (1891)*, *The Old Castle (1893)* and ***The Cloud (1896)***. The castle and gallery added in 1913 are nestled in a magnificent park of hundred year old oaks and large gardens decorated with sculptures by French and Swedish artists, including Auguste Rodin and Carl Milles.

NATIONALMUSEUM

O pened in 1866 in an elegant palace inspired by the Venetian and Florentine Renaissance, the **National Museum** holds the royal collection that Gustav III bequeathed to Sweden. Along with this collection, which includes paintings, objects and tapestries from the 15th century, new acquisitions over the years have made the National Museum the most important museum in Sweden. The edifice, designed by architect August Stüler, overlooks the Strömmen canal and is three stories high. The first floor contains the gallery of carvings, temporary exhibits and the auditorium; the second floor is dedicated to applied arts and design; while the top floor exhibits over 16,000 paintings and sculptures. It includes artists such as Rembrandt (The Batavian Conspiracy, 1661-1662), Rubens, Degas, Renoir, and leading Swedish painters of the 18th, 19th and 20th centuries, including **Anders Zorn (Midsommardans, 1897)** and Alexander Roslin (Woman with Veil, 1769). The sculptures include the Faun (1774), a masterpiece by Johan Tobias Sergels.

MODERNA MUSEET

A naval base until the early 18th century, **Skeppsholmen Island** was later transformed into a tranquil oasis nestled in a park, dotted with some of the largest and most interesting museums in the city. In addition to the **Moderna Museet**, you can visit the **Museum of Architecture** and the Museum of Oriental Art.

The Moderna Museet is a legendary place that has displayed contemporary Swedish and international art since 1958. It has one of the most important collections in Europe and consists primarily of classics in modernism from the entire 20th century to the present, including works by Matisse, Picasso, Dali, Klee, Rauschenberg and many others. In 1998 a new building was opened, designed by the **Spanish architect Rafael Moneo**. Ever-changing exhibits, free admission and a charming restaurant with a magnificent view of the city have made the Moderna Museet a world attraction.

The museum's permanent collections include a significant number of paintings, sculptures, installations, watercolors, drawings, graphic works and photographs.

MUSEUM OF NATURAL HISTORY AND COSMONOVA

*O*n the northern edge of the city, the **Naturhistoriska Riksmuseet** is one of the largest natural history museums in the world, commissioned by Swedish naturalist Charles Linnaeus (1707-1778)

at the time the Academy of Sciences was established. Designed by Axel Anderberg and completed in 1916, the edifice that holds it was restored and expanded in the 1980s and 1990s.

At the same time, the **Cosmonova** was added, with a planetarium and gigantic IMAX screen that shows movies in the world's largest film format.

At the museum entrance is a dark granite obelisk with a ship at the top. The work of sculptor Ivar Johnsson, it was built in 1930 in memory of explorer Adolf Erik Nordenskiöld, who had made a voyage across the Northeast Passage fifty years earlier. The museum is divided into four main sections: the botanical section, with over 4 million species; the zoological section, representing fauna of the world, with arctic species in particular; and the geological and paleontological sections. The exhibit dedicated to Precambrian life includes some dinosaur remains found on Skåne Peninsula in southwest Sweden. The institution's activity includes temporary exhibits, public workshops and seminars, and international research projects.

MILLESGÅRDEN

*A*bout a half hour from the city center, on Lidingö Island, is the estate that once belonged to **Carl Milles** (1875-1955), one of the greatest sculptors of the 20th century. Born in a town near Uppsala, in 1906 he bought 18,000 m2 of land on the island and settled there with his wife, the Austrian painter Olga Granner. In 1936, after moving to the United States, he donated Millesgården to the Swedish people, although he returned there for brief summer vacations until his death. The sculptor's house and studio are now open to visitors, as is the immense terraced garden that extends all around it. The main building is comprised of a small dining room, an elegant gallery with mosaic floor and alabaster

lamps designed by Milles himself, the Music Room, where you can admire various masterpieces from the art collection (a landscape by Camille Pisarro, a view of Corsica by Maurice Utrillo and a 1906 watercolor by Auguste Rodin entitled *Act of Love*), the Red Room, so called due to its Pompeian red walls, which hold some of the sculptor's most significant works, including a bronze depicting a *Water-Nymph Riding a Dolphin* (1918), and the Munich Room, a small room with objets d'art from all over the world. There is also a noteworthy collection of works of art from ancient Greece and Rome that Milles acquired during his trips in Europe, conserved in the long east gallery. A small structure that served as his housekeeper Anna's residence has now been incorporated into the museum, along with the exhibit room designed in 1999 by architect Johan Celsing, which holds displays of Swedish and international art. The real attraction at Millesgården is the Sculpture Park, which contains originals and replicas of Milles' masterpieces. Some of the most famous are *The Venus Fountain with Shell* (1917), the monumental *Fountain of Faith* (1950-52), one of Milles' best-known works, which can be found at the National Memorial Park in Falls Church, Virginia; the **Head of Poseidon** (1930), 7 meters high, with the god carrying a fish and a shell from which cascades of water pour, and the bronze group **Man and Pegasus** (1949), one of Milles' later masterpieces. Another famous monument, with replicas all over the world, is the group entitled *The Hand of God* (1954), the original of which is in the Swedish town of Eskilstuna.

CENTRAL TRAIN STATION

*L*ocated next to the old city and connected to the city center by underground passageways, the **Central Station** was built between 1867 and 1871 based on a design by Adolf W. Edelsvärd. It was refurbished many times, most recently in 1986, when the platforms were covered and a ticket room was added. It was Nils Ericsson, brother of the famous inventor who perfected steamships, who created a design for a railway network in Sweden and advocated a single central station on the north bank of Lake Mälaren. Under his supervision, work went forward quickly: in December 1856 the first stretch of the line between Göteborg and Malmö opened, and in 1862 King Carl XV opened the longest railroad in Scandinavia, connecting Göteborg to the capital.

STOCKHOLM IN WINTER

Ice on Riddarfjärden

City Hall

*W*hile the city enchants visitors in the summer with its long hours of daylight, mild climate, clean water and luxuriant natural setting, Stockholm in winter has a very distinctive charm. Although the days are short, the sun, which seems to lie almost motionless just above the horizon, warmly illuminates the gardens white with snow and the tree branches dripping with pearls of ice. The evenings and long nights are event-filled, especially during the St. Lucy and Christmas celebrations with their beloved traditions. A large outdoor skating rink is opened in the Kungsträdgården, and the picturesque cafes of the old city offer typical sweets and hot chocolate to warm you up.

Stortorget in Gamla Stan

Norrström and the Royal Palace

©: KINA ITALIA / L.E.G.O. - Göran Brämming Gallery AB
Printing: KINA ITALIA / L.E.G.O. - Italy, 2010
Text: Claudia Converso
Translation: A.B.A. - Milano
First published 2006
Published by: Göran Brämming Gallery AB, Stockholm, Sweden
Editorial work: Gunnar Heilborn